edgeland

and other poems

T0307124

the biblical lifespan, the day of feasting, the yesteryear of tomorrows,
the week of peace, the month of giving, the decade of deliverance,
the century of miracles, the eternity of comeuppance, the hour of hope,
time is the nanosecond of download, the instant of reckoning ...

DAVID EGGLETON

edgeland

and other poems

OTAGO

Published by Otago University Press
Level 1, 398 Cumberland Street
Dunedin, New Zealand
university.press@otago.ac.nz
www.otago.ac.nz/press

First published 2018
Copyright © David Eggleton

The moral rights of the author have been asserted.
ISBN 978-1-98-853127-4

Editor: Emma Neale
Front cover: James Robinson, *Utopia's Mines*, 2014, mixed media assemblage, 90 × 75cm.
Interior art: James Robinson. These artworks are from a series entitled 'Drawings', produced by
the artist in 2015 in response to lines from poems by David Eggleton.
Author photograph: Fieke Neuman
Design/layout: Fiona Moffat

Printed in China by Asia Pacific Offset.

CONTENTS

ONE: TĀMAKI MAKAURAU

TWO: MURIHIKU

THREE: SPIDERMOON

FOUR: SCALE

FIVE: LEGEND

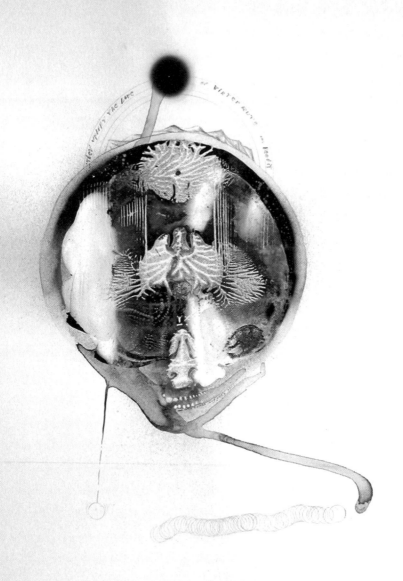

PART ONE: TĀMAKI MAKAURAU

Edgeland

Awks: you winged Auk-thing, awkward, huddling;
you wraparound, myriad, amphibious,
stretchy, try-hard, Polywoodish
juggernaut; you futurescape, insectivorous,
Akarana, Aukalini, Jafaville, O for Awesome,
still with the land-fever of a frontier town –

your surveyors who tick location, location, location,
your land-sharks, your swamp-lawyers, your merchant kings,
your real estate agents who bush-bash for true north,
your architecture that fell off the back of a truck,
your shoebox storerooms of apartment blocks,
your subdivisions sticky as pick and mix lollies;
you fat-bellied hybrid with your anorexic anxieties,
your hyperbole and bulimia, your tear-down and throw-up,
the sands of your hour-glass always replenished,
your self-harm always rejuvenated, unstoppable;
you binge-drinker, pre-loader, storm-chaser,
mana-muncher, hui-hopper, waka-jumper,

light opera queen, the nation's greatest carnivore;
cloud-city of the South Pacific, it's you the lights adore.

Maunga: Volcanoes

High balconies now, these volcanoes were bowls of fire
gathered by Mataaho – Ngā Huinga-a-Mataaho,
out of Te Moana Nui a Kiwa to keep that god warm –
magma erupting from basalt eighty kilometres down.
Rangitoto, the last, emerged a geological breath ago,
on Waitematā's steaming waters, under blood-red skies.

Look-outs for the bellbird and swooping pouākai,
maunga were carved by arriving iwi into palisades,
and food baskets, great earth ramparts, ovens.
On Maungakiekie, warriors streaked with ochre
trampled out haka, breathing to humming bugles
of wood, bound with strong aerial roots of the kiekie.

These hills were given many names. Maungakiekie,
hill of the kiekie plant, became Te Tōtora i Ahua,
hill of the tapu tōtara, or 'One Tree Hill', before
the lone tōtara was cut down for a settler's cottage
in 1853, and replaced by a pine tree.
The settler's family's now extinct; pine's gone too.

At Te Tātua-a-Riukiuta, Three Kings,
were once three cones, mostly quarried away,
and beneath them, sepulchres, tunnels, bones.
All those scoria mountains sheltered bats,
and echoed with water, slipping through the lava
to form wells in caves that siphoned down slopes.

The carver changed the boy into a gecko, the girl to a tree;
and hid the carving in a swamp, drained for a farm.
The burning left ash deposits of touch and taste,
tawa, mānuka, ponga, kahikatea, rimu ablaze,

that singe in memory like a grind of Coromandel
bush pepper, or smoke from scrub on the side of Mt Eden.

Rarotonga was swallowed by Winstone quarry:
Mount Smart stadium stands there, echoing ecstatic fury.
Maungauika is North Head; Maungarei, Mount Wellington,
Puketāpapa, Mt Roskill; Te Kōpuke, part of Epsom.
Around these swollen bellies, hollow gourds of the supercity,
vines coil and constrict with mathematical precision.

The Sleepers

They named the forty-eight sleepers
with names that enshrined imperial purpose,
from Mount Hobson to Mount Victoria,
and made them triumphal arches fallen,
taken away one truckload at a time, so that,
led by the hand, landscape knuckled under
to dirt worked over for foundations of a town.
Governor Grey endowed them as domains,
as 'Mountains' or 'Kings'; and for the pioneers
volcanoes were navigational beacons, but soon
that archipelago, rising from a sea of roofs,
was hollowed, and even levelled. Mounts
Albert and Smart and Wiri Mountain
were shifted beneath the Main Trunk Line
as ballast between Whāngārei and Ōhakune,
or later dumped under the motorway causeway
across the upper harbour. Nothing remains of Ōtara Hill.
Puketutu Island was flattened, pink scoria taken
for Māngere runways, for Jean Batten's aerodrome.
Villages were brought closer to Queen Street,
and each other, by dynamited volcanic rubble
crushed for a base layer of basalt chips over
a sub-base of aggregate – all topped with tarseal.
Concrete pavements and asphalt footpaths
sat on steamrollered clinker, blistered with bubbles.
They built from blue stone the prison, street kerbing,
the barracks, wall boundaries, the police station.
They knocked down timber, built up in basalt.
At the quarry face were gravel-shovelling champions.
Lava flow, gorges ghostly with rain vapour,
became bitumen skeins, tying the suburbs.
Of those forty-eight sleepers, half are gone,
or nearly gone; only Rangitoto has stayed untouched.

The Fencibles

Nimbocumulus floated its flotilla of canvas
spanked above the climacteric of landfall made.
Fencibles were settler-soldiers with families,
their rowlocks grating over the boom of breakers.
As islands within islands, volcanoes brooded.
Stockade posts stared like sentinels, saying nothing,
Fencibles listened to streams feed the marshy reeds.
Water to drink was sweet, filtered through charcoal.
Sun broke like breakfast yolk on streaky rashers of cloud.
There were dugouts, redoubts, raupō whare, logs for paths;
a mud-town of neighing horses, sentinels on parade.
Wooden wheels, iron-rimmed, churned bracken.
Fencibles mused on insects entombed in clear resin;
and bartered with Māori for land and firewood.
The light on gated pastures was rolled gold,
surveyed and mapped and bought and sold.
Bubblers, freshets, trickles grew into Western Springs.
Cairns became forts; colonists replaced the fencibles.
Waka were holed, and the shallows were filled in;
scows, cutters, ketches succeeded by steamships.
Brewers became the old identities; they mattered.
Kauri, pit-sawn, was nailed up as church architecture.
Stockade posts, relics absorbed into the museum;
amber too: lode of mesmerising sunshine of those days.

Two Takes on the Waitākere Ranges

'The hills and mountains are covered in wood and every valley has a rivulet of water.' *Captain James Cook, 1773*

I

Te Waonui-a-Tiriwa, awesome forest of Tiriwa,
with fantails darting up, waterfalls jinking down,
with skinks sidling beneath green mingimingi,
and arcades of fern dropping giddily to the sea:
falling to the tossing white manes of the toetoe,
or rising to rātā's glowing cloak of carmine.
The hollow pūriri are catacombs, and dead fronds
cling to tree-ferns like feathery brown ballgowns.
Deep in gullies, the mānuka is dry, or damp.
Down such a gulch, the last stand was made:
Mahuika's fingernails smouldered, forest crackled.
Charcoal makers admired their handiwork:
a scarred, charred phoenix awaiting rebirth
as mānuka scrubland, exotic shrubs, stoat habitat.

II

Early in the morning, they propped up the stars:
hammered bronze bark stroked by sunlight,
their heartwood a greeny-yellow or light gold,
great cylinders proud to the sky, their crowns
of orchids and moss, cities for aphids, beetles, spiders.
They flourished as the tap-roots of the citadel: kauri.
Those Samsons of timber barons pulled them in,
pillars of the temple, working out the resource,
chapter and verse, chiselled, adzed, milled, rolled;
cradled on wheels of the bush sawyers' railway
to crash, beached, foundered, to be lifted
and dumped without ceremony in a scow,

or rafted, floated, towed en masse to Onehunga
and a fate as flooring, cupboards, desks.

Flying In, Southside

At Māngere the airport welcomes you to Middle Earth,
coasting on a jet's wing and a karakia,
but the industrial parkland unfolds as generic,
though 'nesian mystics harmonise snatches of melody
on Bader Drive by the fale-style churches of Little Tonga,
all the way around the Town Centre to busy PAK'nSAVE,
from whose carpark the Mountain looks back, submerging.

Manaia sail across blue heaven to catch daydreams;
they glide like slo-mo fa`afafine above South Auckland:
the big box stores, all in orange green yellow or red,
as big as aircraft hangars in this polycotton lavalava
wraparound hibiscus paradise of Pap'toe, 'Tara, Ōtāhu –
the Happy Coin marts, the fly-by-night clearance outlets,
the stack 'em high, sell 'em cheap, plastic whatnot bins.

A pearl nacre overcasts closed abattoirs of Southdown,
colonial headquarters of Hellaby's meat empire,
shunting yards of Ōtāhuhu Railway Workshops.
Two-dollar leis sway outside shops on Great South Road.
There's Fiji-style goat curry and Bollywood on screens,
kava, taro, fish heads on ice, hands of green bananas –
no sign of Sigatoka blight amid tart tangelo pyramids.

The suburban origami of bungalow roofs is folded over,
under the warmth of 'Māngere'/'lazy wind': so hot and slow
it barely moves the washing on thousands of clotheslines.
Planes touch down; sirens yammer through the tailbacks;
Macca's golden arches sweat the small hours,
and a police chopper after midnight bugs the sky;
weaving back and forth over quiet streets of Manurewa.

King Tide, Northside

The moon is close, at her perigee, imperious,
summoning the salty fever of a king tide.
Volcanoes seem to change position,
to drift farther out, or drift closer;
and creeks are frothy-mouthed.
What's salvaged from ocean
might splash up on shore,
ferried from creaking timbers anchored well out,
gilding what it covets with a kia ora tātou,
and a good sousing for whatever can be caught.
Tank Farm to Silo Park, they are keeping
their heads up, though boardwalks are lapped.
Paddlers frolic; sand flaunts its wet silks.
Crowds are shoaling like inanga.
The king tide purls on Meola Reef pathway,
and makes a long grab for East Coast Bays,
The king tide casts a net for gasping creatures,
for reclamation of the waterfront,
for the holy scallop of sand in every blessed cove,
knowing that if you cut a thousand metre channel
between Ōtāhuhu Creek and the Manukau Harbour
you could create Aotearoa's third-largest island
to ebb around, searching for wetlands.
And Auckland's flapping like a kahawai,
flapping greeny-blue and silvery,
above all the speckled cockled shelly beaches,
as long-legged girls walk by the creep of the tide,
and the biceps of blokes bulge, hefting a rugby ball.
Pōhutukawa know the king tide well;
they cliff-hang like trapeze artists,
branches parallel to the ground
and demanding elbow room.

They have a ringside seat.
At night, the old soak of the sea
will go rolling rolling rolling home,
dark beneath the phosphorescence of the city.

Tāmaki Drive

Rap thumps its canoe-hauling chant,
from inside a four-wheel drive with tinted windows,
whose engine's reverberant whine
sings the names of Tāmaki's thousand lovers.
The stars are unseen as wet dawn lights
up each type of sea wave and kind of rain
splashing the runnels of each waka, voyaging on.
The land itself is choppy today, rain
smacking the sides of cars trucks vans utes,
that metal cataract pouring through and away.
The compass of the city lurches,
and corrects to the equator,
as warm rain breaks like bowspray
along roads flung like a net around bumps
of an ocean-dwelling taniwha with a slick green shine.

Phantasmagoria from Mount Victoria/ Takuranga, Devonport

On an autumn morning, tall buildings bulk
like war canoe prows, while foghorns moan
to warn that out there boxy container ships skulk.
In sea chambers, vapour condenses into foam,
ghosts shadowy and bodiless form from mist,
and sailors' tattoos seem to wreathe and twist.
The metal of the Harbour Bridge bends like a bow,
Moller's half-seen Sky Tower could be its arrow.
A Shore ferry trembles to cleave through water,
backwash thrashing like some snared albatross.
From Takuranga's top you see a contained harbour,
hemmed by filmy webs, wet paspalum, whiteness.
Dog-walkers are glimpsed; anglers have vanished.
Each island's a whaleback: the Gulf's lathered.

Hauraki

Dark as flax cloaks stained with ash is the isthmus.
Fast thunderheads dim the evershifting light's pulse.
A howly bag of weeping winds and drunkard gusts
hurries in from Hauraki Gulf to empty holus-bolus
rain squalls from Kawau Island to the Hunuas.
First dull spit, then steady spots, then drops in surplus.
Hinewai's the light rain, Te Ihorangi the monsoon colossus –
in crescendo, like Pasifika drummers felt in the solar plexus.
Dragging their sousing trains, the holy rains process.
Dog bowls runneth over; quick-time car wipers make a fuss.
Pavements are eel alleys; roads are wheke tentacles –
they fling out and grip as suckers of a great octopus.
Rain prods earthworms in darkness to rise from humus,
emerging on Eden Park's turf to writhe exultant, tremulous.

Day Swimmers

Playing a blinder, pinions of oars swinging,
high pressure across the Tasman.
Shiny dinghies wobble on the shiny water,
and a single cloud floats in the oceanic blue.
The sensurround is all sea, the sea all street;
but inland's marine too, stripped to shipboard weather,
bright-eyed in gloss and sun-damaged fabric.
Inlets are graced by mangrove top-knots, ribbed sandbars,
and nīkau palms, ponga ferns, vine tangles.
The Waitematā's on tap today, the Gulf's a view,
where everyone's spooning up guzzles of light
everlasting from saggy verandahs of wooden villas,
perpetual fermentations of a home-brewed fizz
that brings out bathers raring to go, who plunge
and become heads bobbing in cauls as they cleave
an oceanic saltiness, but hugging the shore.
Far out, jelly stingers trail tendrils, sea-gloom made rapt
by plankton's bling beneath plough-keels of yachts.
Cicadas chorus in parks at fever pitch.
Soon, burgeoning meringues of cumulus will darken,
rococo cream puffs dunked in thunderheads.
A rain-burst will roll in with dazzle-bright drops.
Later, the song of the grasshopper, pale greenstone;
and from hedges at night, zit-zit goes the katydid.

The Floral Clock

Dawn's orange soak rinses gently the copper lid
that floats over Noel Lane's big kava bowl
back of the War Museum and the front's white colonnade,
and Ferro-Concrete Company's Grafton Gully bridge span;
and Albert Park, too, where a floral clock used to grow,
and Sir George Grey was beheaded one Waitangi Day.
Great War's planted trees are in leaf round Victoria Park,
glorious, but nearby the trees nurse amputated limbs.
Dawn bathes the foxed map of Rudyard Kipling's lovely ark:
city of Three Lamps, College Hill, the Viaduct rush,
of New World supermarket, standing where tanks
of gasworks and the town's brick incinerator
once stood proud on the flat in Freemans Bay –
after reclamation, for everything's on the move –
only slower than dawn as it strikes Micky Savage's Tomb,
and the diamond-shaped panes of Saint Mary's Church,
drawn up by Benjamin Mountford for Bishop Selwyn.
At Britomart, sun's on the fountain, the hanging garden,
on grooves left by saw-teeth on wine bar beams.
Sun's on the ferry building's disembarkations,
strikes the wharfies, seagulls, off-loading boats,
straddle-carriers, laden trays of truck after truck.
Sun's on Ellerslie Racecourse and Newmarket Flyover;
glances along discharge pipes near New Lynn.
Gongs of empty waste bins vibrate at noon;
solar panels on rooftops flare with light;
and Waikumete angels contemplate headstones,
whose shadows lengthen like sundials.

Two Prospects

I

Prospect of Ponsonby

Someone lifts a sash window to admit the spectacle.
Squelchy, abandoned, lush beyond propriety,
windfall plum undertones and mint grace-notes,
bamboo, nasturtiums, arum lilies, jasmine,
kikuyu grass, privet, thistle,
grapefruit tree, lemon tree, chicken wire,
frangipani, magnolia, fennel, a rusty pram,
creepers, vines, daffodils, onion flowers,
ragwort, all crowd the mesmerising sunshine.
Gardeners itch to get amongst it:
old prospect of Ponsonby, invisible to most.
Back of the daffodils, locals are planting natives.

II

Prospect below the Mount

Shadows trapped in panes of glass, reflective windows
frame spruced up villas amid salads of shrubbery,
crammed earthenware. Kōwhai is in flower.
Rain patters theatrical sudden applause.
Dodge out of the humid, earth-smelling cloudburst,
and inside, the other Eden's a mall: automatic doors
open like rock fissures into franchised calm,
and the roar of raindrops settles down to soft muzak.
Leaving there the light strikes so hibiscus hedges glitter.
A quick breeze gallivants the air from blue sky haka.
Teenagers yomp skateboards across the skate-park.
A butterfly extends frail wings and sails to a tree palm.

Methusalem

Shame, a flame-red flush,
the scowling darkness hisses –
thunder rumble and bolts thrown
to the electric attraction of opposites,
their mutual sickness,
holding a relationship together
with resonant frequencies.
He said, she said, they said, on the salty wind –
salt mines of the crystal field,
text blinking on the blue wand
that the eye scans.
July's vibrating electro-magnetic field,
oscillating in step, humming in sympathy,
shadowy frequencies joining in,
with infra-dig, ultra-violet, X-ray ring
tones to set up a stone blackout.

In damped under-awnings,
invisible colours revealed,
that ricochet to the blueing of distant hills,
thick vapours on the Waitākeres,
blue butterfly wings almost,
as scales that shimmer sea-green,
and shift on the wing,
gold, sapphire, emerald show offs,
wing-wavers,
grinding and scattering in mounds, dunes, heaps,
fills, pulled from earth,
discovered, uncovered, chameleon.

We sink into Auckland and live here,
its resonances,

its lane-bending dreams, grey and colourless,
then blooming with colour,
compounds of lead springing forth
as white-lead weatherboard, red-lead iron,
painting refrangible bull's-eye Auckland.
Auckland, oh yes, its arbitrary
subdivisions
of the sunlit spectrum –
its harmonies of rooftops,
its bignesses, its hulking monster stingray,
its flounder stuck to mud beds,
its blue deepening to purple,
its indigo and violet bruises,
its blood-letting,
its streets that smack you
in the face with their indifference,
its crowds that sing to many different
notes and chords, its road hogs.

A clear noise of vehicles and call signs,
mobiles and radios,
sunlight silent in the echo
of post-festival euphorias,
multi-pitched Babel cosmos
of compressed continents through voices
urgent to be heard,
and sunlight falling silent as smog particles
drifting into canyons,
beauteous curves of smoothed-out gullies
running seaward.
The frozen berries sing, and the black bitumen
splits to reveal gravel baby teeth,
the rule of thumb guided along the dotted line,
where they split the atom and peered inside,
logos, eros, budding forth.

The tents of green are gathered here,
in muddied brilliance
of rainbow refractions inside droplets.
The huddles in a darkened care
home are ancient McCahon hills
under brown and black blankets,
and there's white from Moana's necklace
and white from Rangi's cloak,
and there's red from pōhutukawa
and red from bark and soil –
rust-red, burgundy, russet on the rainbow spectrum,
hazel, chestnut, the ardour of ochre,
and an oily pond, wine-dark, in a glass.

Those moist, cool greens on an Auckland
winter suburban morning,
amid gemstone tail-lights –
the malls that suck up moisture,
and spring it in rainbow-coloured arcs
through a plastic straw
between strawberry slush lips.
Plastic is a shattering of the unity
of sulphur, mercury, chlorophyll, blood,
into separate lotions, elixirs, potions, cordials,
into liniment's spirit blackout in the July city.
Plastic was the future,
in orange, pink, yellow, ultramarine,
in ivory, copper, cinnamon, maroon,
in bright, dark, heavy, light blue,
in fifteen blues,
and so the colour field grew.

Now's the muddied brilliance
of flesh, drapery, water, shelter,
in this fool's paradise of prismatic arcs,

this July city –
clouds a purple-dyed wool piled on benches,
and streaked crimson and vermilion,
smeary as dashed dregs of coffee,
as clotted blood darkly reflected.
The storm closing in, like a border patrol,
with heads of dark rose, foams of dark grape,
a blue-dark pompadour,
fists tattooed by a bruise-dark manifesto.

The blood is sewn together
to float as a fine rain
against high windows and spires,
and above Karangahape,
so see you on the other side
of the underpass, the passing over,
above Karangahape –
its greenish-tinged billboards,
its blue boundaries dissolving.
The blue riders on the storm,
plunging and rearing in foams and sea salt,
in table-top clutter, in bundles of vegetables,
that are rain-soaked greener black,
blackened wet by the storm –
its indigomania, its sapphire flash,
its blitz of threads carrying across
azure the blue of the underworld,
the mauve movements of cloud banks.

Colours running into rainbow darks,
into silver tarnishes and blurs,
into neon's noodle swirls,
into woodgrain vinyl, and painted dirt.
Soakage overwriting blades of grass
with new particulars, with each thing numbered,

with mashings of leaves and barks –
druggists sifting for drugs with a sieve
to strain into reservoirs,
to press out the juices, to knead
the pulp of all the parks,
in midnight shades with vivid blue flashes,
strident hues bleached by headlamps,
a rich umber of landslips for the new day –
and the July city at midnight wobbling
its hundreds and thousands of dots,
like the glow of a bush fire far away.

IN CREMATORIA

ME
MEMEME
MB
MB
MB
MB
BY DAVID ESHAUGHNESSY

MY CYCLONE UNEARTHS A SACRED LATIKIN
MY BOOM WATER STAGNATES IN BELGIAN ZIGGURATS
MY BOOK OF SCRIBBLY GUM OPENS ON FIREBOMBS

MY MILL OF ASHES SEETHS LIKE A FRENZIED CALIPHATE

MY CRACKED GLASS SMOKES OUT A SEASON OF ARSONISTS
MY YELLOW MONDAY CRACKLES WITH PAYBACKS CLAMOUR
MY BLANK TV SCREEN BLACK AS CELEBRITY SHADES CONCENTRATES GLEAMS WAITS FOR RECOGNITION
A SPONTANEOUS IGNITION OF DAYTIME SOAPS MY TRUE HORIZON DANCES ON BLOW TORCHED PICASSE
THE SCAMMED TO SWING DOWN LIKE JAILBAIT
MY DRY STACK BURSTS OUT FROM A LIGHTENING TOSS
MY SCRUB EXPLODES ON HIGH BEAMS OF HEAT OTHER COLOURS BURN WHITE AS
TO ELECTRIC

PART TWO: MURIHIKU

Lake Wakatipu

A jade lizard bends in a circle,
chasing its tail;
straightens, and darts for a crevice.
Mist swathes in grey silk the lake:
flat-stomached, calm, slow-pulsed,
a seamless bulk.
Vapours spiral,
pushing up to a cloud-piercer,
where snow has been sprinkled
like powder from a talc can at height.
Grandeur stands muffled.
The *Earnslaw* headbutts shorewards.
After lying prone for years,
rocks shift downwards
at speed, eager to wheel
through air, crash in a gully,
and not move.
The lake buttons up to dive deep,
leaving a perfectly blank black space,
through which you might fall forever.

Distant Ophir

I went looking for the nightingale,
for the rose, and found corrugated iron,
scent of wild thyme, cry of a hawk.

I felt a breeze lift in the orchard,
to waken the leaves from slumber
and entangle memories in apricot heat.

Monday was washday, Tuesday ironing,
Wednesday cleaning, Thursday baking,
Friday shopping, Saturday sports games.

Sunday meant church, promise of roast dinner.
Air stood dry and warm beneath pine trees.
Crickets leapt over sunflower radiance.

Summer's elixirs glistened in green jelly.
Jam was given in peach and cherry.
Quicksilver sank in the foxed mirror.

The breeze, a stir of quiet fingers,
plucked at floury puffs of petals,
fluffed sponge cake, buttered big scones.

Furniture stacked, empty windows blank,
fine bones showing, faded curtains folded,
the farmhouse went for a knockdown price.

If I peer hard now through the late afternoon,
I can almost see as far as distant Ophir,
and cargo from Otago, raising the dust.

Saddle Hill

Hill stuck in land's lift,
hill bowed under coach-and-horses southerly,
beneath flung clods of cloud,
and lightning rod's crackle.
Hill of a darkening domestic blue,
where tresses of a tree
are caught by wind's plough,
by a sidelong slope ripple,
and state highway sidle
in winding bitumen.
Hill staunch as fence of number eight wire,
staunch as a moa's haunch in a bog,
or a Land Rover driven up Mount Cook.
Hill of the earth, raggedy-as,
that shrugs and scrubs up a little higher
with rain's sleek gurgle,
hill like some spavined nag wanted for glue,
bound on a cross-country canter
towards plains, where the dairy cow
and small-town mayors battle.
Hill telescoped and named by James Cook,
sailing in the eighteenth century,
for a horse saddle.
Hill clambering now a slumped dome,
dug-away, quarried megaphone
trumpeting change,
over which jets hurtle
north for the big smoke.

Spinners

Marsh grasses flap like a magic carpet,
ready to fly; ripples crank across water;
lifted seeds, skerricks, beetle husks, ping.
The bracken's eiderdown floats.
Punished hair farmers thumb a ride
with sheaves of pummelled tussock.
Slow white blades chop at airy nothing.

Weather loosens stones on a hill.
A townie, I drift by tarn and lichen,
pitched up on a rock parabola,
as turbines below lift angelic wings
and a cogwheel momentum turns,
zap-zap in revolution to tame hurly
burly, a quickening when isobars tighten.

Bone blade, shadow stalker, skylark trill,
a hawk soars to let fall a feathered kill.
In wind's eye, a child's windmill on a stick
hangs motionless till flippers fiercely flick.
The dervishes whirl their arms in bedlam:
giant spirits droning lung-burst stanzas,
prayer hum blown away in electric bonanzas.

Tūhawaiki, the Catlins

Jack's Blowhole: twenty minutes there, twenty back,
across an impassive mass of cliff faces,
to the tiny platform built on chopped out rock.
Loud crump, whistling 'Dixie' like a steam loco,
full speed ahead, ocean with a pāua sheen
races with turbine force, till thar it blows.
Your whale spout our breath, your tide our thread,
your door our wall, your sea cave our expulsion.
Surge that forever labours, cathedral builder,
stone pounder, hanging foam along the coast.

A flock of spoonbills climbs into summertime.
On a fence, one hundred pig hides, slung to dry.
Above the turquoise swell hang thunderheads,
black as bargeboards charred to the waterline.
Driftwood rides surf like a bowsprit's figurehead,
then is dunked under, then is resurrected.
Bladderwrack slithers to flail away at the rip.
Wind skates ocean with the serene speed
of waka paddlers, whose blades dip and plunge,
their craft flying to Bloody Jack's chanted rhythm,
as in a vision carried to Hone Tuwhare
by a kākā from the river's mouth near Ōwaka.

A beach bonfire blaze catches at sunset.
Its sparks, scoured from the bowl of the bay,
whirl up to anchor themselves in the sky.
Braided with lichens, a stand of trees darkens.
Salt water widens over brindled sand,
and reflects the glitter of far-off galaxies.

Southern Embroidery

A killjoy's claw, a feathered dawn,
the liar's tripwire that traps birdsong;
a hawk's lunge, a car's speed,
magnetic mountains burning white.
Turquoise lake; skeletal rock clack
to sound the glooms of algal blooms,
freak-out traverse, funky forest floor,
blood-hot springs and hail's cool millions.
A rainbow sifts gravel for colour.
Rusty prayer wheels of seagulls turn.
The whale's maw pulls everything in,
while octopus tentacles with motion seek
sudden fanfares of dolphin whistles.
Sooty shearwater flocks crowd the sky:
drawn black thread, thicker and thicker.
On a single breath float moon and feather.

Tourists Everywhere

Travelling down
the long, rotting log of the West Coast,
over moss, over stone,
cameras hunt for great white mountains,
shutters whirring,
at pointed teeth sharking into blue skies.
In the foreground,
trees lean together against wind
that carries the sound
of the sea surge shunting
and shouldering amongst
boulders of the beach.

The Wilder Years

Us, with our sewing, quilting, plumbing bees,
going hard yakker till the eleventh hour,
we'll be throwing on the barbie one more sacred cow,
and tossing the hoons mallowpuffs and macaroons
to keep them bemused between beers,
then hosing it all down with tanker milk.
A clinking canticle of glasses is poured
as all Kiwiland gets on board –
in sheep's clothing looking wolfish, a teeth-gnashing nation.

These shaky isles of geyserland porridge,
wind gusts and snow, and blinding sunshine
spread like butter on the bread of the mundane,
show all the blue, blue days of shunted livestock
are otherwise fine, so get in behind, ya mongrels.
You can, in this country, walk on water,
so long as you don't rock the boat,
but always speak the truth and always shut the gate.

How we yearn to be lost and found on shores
of islands loveliest, loneliest, fierce and raw,
though often rent asunder by thud and blunder,
and sometimes by pillage and plunder,
running down the mountainous spine,
where greenstone's a hollow pampered jade,
and pounamu jiggles on a piece of string.
Flag, anthem, dairy herd, rugby team identity
are carried on the narrow back of the new Hawaiki,
to the jeers of old-time mountaineers
whose core-sample memories are all that remain
of a rattletrap past wrapped in its own bombast,
its own jars of extract of sticky black yeast.

Twice branded by the slash-mark of Zorro,
Enzed is machine washable and in a state of global warming.
Enzed is delirium tremens, too, a trigger warning.
Enzed is a mega uplift junket, a berm with a view,
a watchamacallit, Lotto prize, gold-plated thrill,
a hoiho five-spot, mōhua hundie, kārearea kill,
a folding koha, whio blue duck, ten dollar bill.

Game

Mud-cracked, mud-punked, mud-brindled,
each foot unplugged from montane bogs,

they are tackled in mud, and then some,
strugglers sliding to the splash of try-line.

They catch the future, turn it over in their hands;
then down they scrum, with mud-flecked faces.

Again they fall, as if thrown to the very bottom,
held down in the muddy slither of trenches.

Climbing up again through troughs of rain,
they are the whole earth, kicking for touch.

Scenery Muncher

So the mountains have been in labour,
and given birth to the scenery muncher –

the face of a possum, the stealth of a stoat,
the directionlessness of a rabbit,

the bleat of a goat, the plod of a dairy cow.
Silent forests through which ferrets scuttle,

then rats, soon cats, next the browsing herd.
Slow-gaited, low-weighted, udder-baited,

across breadth of a paddock's slime-green dark,
follow-my-lead lines walk to the milking shed.

Above fence-wire horse-high, bull-strong, pig-tight,
hangs a frosty night poetry of stars and baahs.

Sheepish blokes claim that it's just not cricket –
the white shirt plummet from the snowy summit.

The horns of Kenworths are rudely honking,
at the fair go gone from the promised deal.

The tuatara in the green room is on zoom.
A butterfly's broken on a logging truck wheel.

Macca sign whanged by shots from a twenty-two.
Making a fluffy sponge demonstrated by a rugby guru.

Crickets are stridulent at summer's myrtle rust.
An old family bathtub is taking on Cook Strait.

Grizz in the drizzle flips the crowd the bird,
thrown from here to breakfast by eruptions of the absurd.

Kettle

Gumboot, smoky gunpowder,
dried tea that grew
on rich, warm earth.

In kitchen's dawn gleam,
tea at the still point
of a turning world.

For snuggled bedfellows,
estranged by dreams,
tea leaves darken hot water
to the very end of steam.

Over cups of tea, we peer
at morning's blackened toast.

Poured cups of tea, sympathetic
vibrations of a heart to heart.

His forehead shines,
a polished teapot:
he's making tea,
amid crusty sauce bottles.

A storm brews
in the chink of china mug,
the tinkles of a teaspoon.

On a rainy afternoon,
she's marooned,
with a packet of macaroons,
and endless cups of tea.

In the last tea-room in town,
conversations about tea stains;
stale cake crumbs on doilies.

Teetotallers are slurping
through ancient dentures,
back when tea was tuppence,
served in Crown Lynn cups.

A cup of tea on the deck,
a cup of tea on the run,
a cup of tea in the past.

MY CYCLONE UNEARTHS A SACRED LARRIKIN.

PART THREE: SPIDERMOON

New Year's Day at Byron Bay

I'm older now at Byron Bay,
rediscovering its tourist schemes,
while clarity pours from crest to crest,
serenely leading the chasing wash.
The summer crowd loves the whoosh.
It bobbles wet-backed till it gleams,
sunk thigh-deep in the seethe of New Year's Day,
holy for Australians and the Kiwi,
rising drenched from crystal glow,
a roll-on spiced, jasmine, sunblock gloss,
as the human wrack shimmers away
to a haze of sea-meadow,
where sharks cruise like submarines.

In starry Jesus hair streams,
a goofy-foot walks a water-quake.
A foaming breaker drapes his shoulder.
He flips upside-down through a mirror,
then kicks for the blue light,
kicks to where the rip curl lifts
over his ears its redeemer's shower.
The ocean glitter's a soft icing his board planes,
and blue his cloud-swallowing dreams,
bound in foamy loops, whisked to gold's height
for a sponge cake the sun might bake,
He's the jackpot casino winner who preens.
Kids pound the waves with their fists.

In Byron, the anointed test the sunbeams.
Above swamps where crocodiles lurk,
car engines idle, waiting for fossil fuel.
Heat sneaks in and fingers everything,

making greasy marks, while I watch
from a pricey beer balcony
the hippy bus going to Nimbin,
and poolside aquacade teams,
and shoppers whose branded backpacks
hold the globe. Motorists fume
in traffic serpents at the roundabouts.
Their cars growl, having drunk truth serum.
Tourists raise melting ice-creams.

Moreton Bay

When it's stinking hot at twelve o'clock,
earthy aromas rise and vent.
Something's conjured in a gutbucket
and tossed bloodily in a wok
to quarrel with a guzzle of noodles.
Somewhere, someone faces the chop,
gets the elbow, and, down in the mouth,
thumbs the nose like a clothes peg.
The pineapple factory clanks;
a rock melon's guts ferment,
spilled on grease-trap spikes.
Op shop fabrics swelter.
Crow's caw lays down the law.
Fibrolite freedoms let draughts in.
A tin roof's holed like a colander,
shotgunned with sun's dust.
Shacktown's galvanised iron creaks
beneath clatter of fangs, claws, beaks.
Pelicans roost on rusty bridge posts.
Moreton Bay fig trees engage
in elephantine creep.
Against crinkle-eyed seawater,
freckled knuckles row a dinghy out.
Still as a lizard, a man fishes
at evening for a plume of white stars
to answer the day's long thirst.

Spidermoon

The spidermoon burns
reddish-yellow yolky,
sleepwalking through night fields,
a spinner's tranced orb.
Trapezes drift on silk bolas.
Strands carry them a long way
to spokes, sticky spirals,
guyed trapdoors.
Wakefulness in shadows at dawn;
soft, quivering snuffle of a muzzle
nosing grass and bat urine:
the dog's off the chain.

The bombora of Mount Chincogan
tips a green wave down to the yoga church,
and the amped-up ukulele player,
who busks for coins outside the IGA
with 'Yes, We Have No Bananas'.
The check-out chick pops her bubblegum.
Lorikeets squabble beyond the library.
A parrot-man coaxes:
his shoulders are perches.
A galah oohs and aahs.
He feeds the bird clinging to him.
The flock beats wings to a harbouring.

Summer kneads trees
the colour of a bloodnut hamadryad.
Sunflowers glow more yellow
than fluffy sponge-cake.
Cicadas swing like pendant earrings.
Grasshoppers like fallen clothes pegs, leap.

Brush turkeys stalk a picnic sandwich.
Tiny lizards pause, scuttle, pause.
A goanna hotfoots it
over the brickwork of the barbie.
The hot tin roofs
make with their creaking cha-cha.

The air's dry as a dog biscuit.
Stones clang under dusty cars.
The burning tar sports a shiner.
A water dragon's clean-bowled,
spread across the road.
The bat some kid shot at
hangs by claws from a wire.
Birds twitter, rayed out
against the phone transmitter.
The sun's hard-boiled in its shell.
A spinnaker of cloud gets the wind up,
and bolts for the wild blue yonder.

Panel Beater

A high-maintenance, G20 Sky Father.
A desalinised, compostable, home-birther.
A granular plastic skin with vents and grafts.
A bug-eyed and hernia-sprung wobble-board.
A gall wasp, sawfly, slug and aphid display shield.
An age-hardened, unleavened, half-eaten, spiced bun.
An earworm filthy as Lord Melbourne's waistcoat.
A great wombat the colour of tainted coffee-whitener.
A large bowel collider facing early-onset nothingness.
A heavy metal bombardment of daylight bulbs.
A Day of Penitence, factory-farmed, tooter the sweeter.
A camouflaged, eye-patched god-shaped hole.
A whack-a-mole clay and burnt alabaster jackpot.
A sluggish, backwards-compatible, zodiac wheel.

This Gubberment, Bro, This Gubberment

They clown-troupe in for core meltdown goals,
solar flare on tandoori oven's fiery coals,
untouchable dragon-mouth's pizza topping,
burnt ends stitched back up with string.
Choose marinaded redneck flambé dressed with lard,
pig-ear sambo with Rwandan Dukunde Kawa brew,
or the paint, paper, hair, fingernails, cockroach feast.
The second swig of Tanqueray with Angostura,
beslobbered and besmeared on ice-cold rocks;
electric maraschino cherries and shit-eating grin.
Blood runs down the fishy scaling knife,
red as the bled heart of the blessèd saviour
in a flyblown frame made of sticking plasters.
The lunatics have taken over the asylum-seekers.

Penny Serenade

Penny Serenade's jammed in her busted jukebox,
with top-drawer knives, forks, cracked dinner plates;
and here come the exoplanets, the orbiting rocks.
Twelve steps below Paradise, they open the floodgates
to enmesh all in chook-wire and holy ectoplasm.
Mother Earth Normal's now Mother Earth Abnormal,
and software precogs exploit everywhen's shrapnel.
Helicopter parents have the price of a Buddha stick;
their vinyl fetish costumes shine like an oil slick.
Doofus leads the slo-mo exit from Olympus.
I'll asphyxiate you, croon the car fumes,
giving rivers of metal the Anthrocene blues.
You're beautiful in marble, beautiful in mud,
but you're choking, Mother Earth, in fossil fuel crud.

Planet Blast

No poppies blow, they faded long ago,
in potter's field with paupers, job-seekers,
kicked to the curb by bigcorp motorcades.
Brands grow strands of web that loop the planet.
Tiny spider-peeps make raids with tiny lasers:
crap terraforming, global bad positioning.
They uplift the love of Wintermute and feed it
to a novabomb that irradiates the quantum:
our big dumb object beamed from outer space,
each sarcophagus built by a civilisation gone.
So we cling to a death-star collapsium,
our heartbeats those of bug-eyed monsters.
An earthling's cooee echoes under ruptured crust.
We live for earth's breath, like the wind, the dust.

Land Smasher

Gotta have magnets for cleaning out cows.
Cows can swallow bits of wire, and they can kill,
because they drill, they drill into the heart.
Gotta have a rusted, busted, done and dusted
Holden Kingswood, so you can rock up, low
to the ground, dry spinifex stuffed in your tyres.
Gotta have roo mince to feed the dogs.
Gotta have diggers to get the ore from mines.
Gotta dump the dispossessed outside casinos:
those bushland nomads, they don't know they're born.
And keep them boat people on the never-never.
You think I'm pathetic, non-empathetic?
I swerve for possums, so get out of the car,
or fair serve – I swings the iron bar.

In Crematoria

My cyclone unearths a sacred larrikin.
My boom water stagnates in beer can ziggurats.
My book of scribbly gum opens on firebombs.
My mill of ants seethes like a frenzied caliphate.
My cracked glass smokes out a season of arsonists.
My Yellow Monday crackles with payback's clamour.
My blank TV screen, black as celebrity shades,
concentrates its gleams and waits for recognition:
the spontaneous ignition of daytime soaps.
My true horizon dances on blow-torched grasses.
My dry storm bursts out of the slammer,
to swing down like jailbait from a lightning tree.
My scrub explodes on high beams of heat,
white as; other colours burn to electricity.

Heat

Heat wears the head of a kangaroo,
and scarred leather apron with a pouch.
Heat shrink-wraps blood, guts and glory
into the stew of a tossed-out meat pack,
on which a live fur of insects sprouts.
Heat reveals testimony, and unpeels
insect scribbles of a paperbark story.
Heat clangs a rusted-up tap dead.
Heat tastes eucalyptus on the wind.
Heat stuffs the rump of the outback
into a slow cooker from a gunny sack.
Heat dries plumage to desert sand.
Heat throws a dry-course curse
on mongrel margins, and worse.
Heat puts a stop to green leaf-claws.
Heat places a frog's song on the slide.
Heat causes a koala's clutch to contract.
Heat bends metal to sword-blades,
slashes zero and zed on rusted hulls.
Heat lets ashes of forest offerings
settle on towels along the beaches.
Heat wobbles the whole seaboard.
Heat sends the shimmer of a jogger
springing away fast as a kangaroo,
from road stop-lights stuck on red,
in search of rain's cool wherewithal.

Mullum Rain

A frog in a dry downpipe booms
a didgeridoo dirge to welcome
rain's beginning beat and sway.
Another frog calls for calm.
Beetles are clapping. Cicadas screech.
Ant swarms ignore draggled bird song.

After the long dry spell, ozone rises,
tasting of lichen, moss, sativa smoke,
eucalyptus, peppermint, ginger spice rust.

Newly oceanic, each globe revolves,
slides along a leaf, then drops frantic
to reach a mouth, any mouth.

Rainmakers seed clouds with dreams
that braille and blip and slash down.
The clouds put up their sheets of rain
for the wind to blow them down again.

Water from wires wobbles on tangled wash,
black powder ash, pink petals squashed,
fin flash, greyish flecked backwaters,
rolling breakers, rockaway swells.
Warm rain flows over fish scales, black wetsuits,
sea-salted air, birthed sacs, rinds strewn.
Where sap trickles, sudden freshets of rain again,
pell-mell over pulped grains, tree-bark storm-blue.

Mullum dives, hanging tight, a bubbled wraith.
Growth spurts put out tendrils and tongues.
Ponds give suck to sprouting tadpoles.

Slimy underbellies slide from flooded drains.
Slow-bellied, low-bellied, drains emptied fill again.
Swollen slow and low, skies ebb their tide-beat drone.
Ink-well spills scrawl green on faded green.
Jelly water sets in moulds of olive-drab.
Emerald creatures slither and ooze, or wait.

Glossy as embers, carbuncles, brake-lights blink;
gutters stream like data to a smartphone.
Rains perpetual, rains brazen that wink
in undertow of slosh and drown,
in moisture sweating, in mephitic miasmas.

The dirt rain, the gravel rain, the stone rain,
the eel rain, the toad rain, the snake rain,
the hay rain, the worm rain, the herd rain.

Shoelaces, roots, tentacles feel for the slippery.
Pupae, diatoms, prawns, a whole whale,
might swim down, whole mountains float free.

The morning rain that foams like carpet cleaner.
The refreshing rain that soaks laundry liquid.
The pure rain that droops like shower stall soap.
The granite rain making its real estate bid.

You listen to this rain,
this rain listens to you,
fades away then lifts gently;
again beats, hard, spiteful.
Spirited rain that shoals and shawls.
You must dodge the scooped run-off, where it falls.
Rainy day, rain all day, sang Jimi to his stoned guitar.

And doggedly the rain follows us around.
Mullumbimby rain, in a river town.

Melbournia

Horizon's level stared down, we land.
Farm tractors are hoeing corduroy wale.
The air's wrapped in buttered yak wool.
Aboard a bus blatting the Freeway
along kilometres of Tullamarine
towards the keeper of gravity's centre,
place swings low. Laminated by myth,
place has name recognition and reptile skin.
Smellburn, malworm, who apostrophises
marbellous bulb-melt but Ern Malleybin?

Melburnia is charged like a furnace
with trowelled on, just breathable, warming.
The heartbeat of the goanna beats
in the throat of the digger, beats gilded
in the bar, in transports of shimmer,
this place at the edge of a debit card.
Powdered green tea is stirred to a sheen.
Orchids are fragrant, and do not droop.
Rainbow vapours are spritzed from gum oils;
a café's *Exodus* theme is knocked for a loop.

When you rise to the surface of the street,
there comes another drama-school crowd,
with the boom-crash opera of each life
cannonaded star-wards, the shape of each
life rippling with scars, the hurried punters
defrosting conversations from slicked phones.
Their city shines with gold oozing from pores,
a brooding sense of watchfulness wary
above layers of clinker brick, sky like lava.
For each trade-off there is a burden to carry.

Angles monitor themselves. Allure lattices
hawk mysteries blown up to a grand scale.
Buffets of breeze serve as sustenance.
Place feels apocalyptic; needle rays burn
with a fireship sun's smouldered heat,
only refreshed by the air-con in malls.
When walking is a mode of knowledge,
those who wear the sandals of Hermes
must always recite a hot yoga mantra,
or the glare will gouge out their eyes.

At the interchange, exchange kosher Maccas
for halal Maccas, for gluten-free Maccas,
for vegan stew of the polyglot melting pot.
Some are spading plates of mud cake,
others are chopping kebabs with swords.
The lost temper is for crying out loud,
hoisted on thin shoulders of a huggy heroine.
Rubber pummels top seal; the trams amaze you;
tripwires run and twang; sirens sing to streets;
pyres of armoured cockroaches face erasure.

Behind grilles lurks a wilderness of corridors.
Fans in suburbs cool their beatitudes.
Poodle claws clatter on the parquet.
Melancholy twists round with saturnine leer,
where Melbourne mopes, clutching its lanes,
its bunkers hedged about with floribunda.
The city aurora glows, a smog mosaic dome.
Down nerve lines of gliding rails pulses light,
with taste of smoke, diesel oil and ozone.
Bulb-melt's horizon climbs the immense night.

NO POPPIES BLOW THEY FADED LONG AGO. IN POTTED FIELDS WITH PAIN JOB SEEKER
KICKED TO THE CURB BY BIG CORP MORTGAGED BRANDS, GROW STRANDS OF WEB
TINY SPIDER DEEDS MAKE RAID WITH TINY LASERS, CRAP TO AFGOMINI GLOBAL BAD POSITIONING
THEY UPLIFT THE LOVE OF WINTER MUTE AND FEED IT TO A NOLA BOMB THAT EXPLODES
OUR AIR DEEDS OBVERT ELBAINED FROM OUTER SPACE, EACH SARCOPHAGI BUILT BY THE QUANTUM
SO WE CLING TO DEATH STAR COLLAPSIVE. OUR HEART BEATS THAT OF BOY EYES MONSTER GONE
A EARTH UNI LOOSE UNDER A RUPTURED CRUST. WE LIVE FOR EACH BREATH THE WIND SEC

PART FOUR: SCALE

Moa in the Mātukituki Valley: A Cento

Mountains crouch like tigers, resentful,
and Moa's seeking eyes grow blind,
upstream, wading towards the taniwha.

Moa's a strange bird, old and out of time,
driven from the bush by the Main Trunk Line.
The world is divided between Moa and the rest.

Moa, you are not valued much in Pig Island,
though it admires your walking parody,
and poor saps poeming to the trees imitate your malady.

Moa's a good keen citizen, very earnestly digging
in puggy clay at the bottom of the garden for a worm.
Moa cracked a word to get at the inside.

Here come the clouds, Moa, puffy like breasts of birds.
Blue's the word for the feeling, Moa, as you levitate,
homing in on living here with your little flock of sheep.

But, Moa, if you feel you need success,
and long for a good address, don't anchor here
in Pig Island, take a ticket for Megalopolis.

Moa's solitude: pacing along an empty beach,
creating in his head a plan to get at the wild honey.
The door flaps open like a wing; Moa enters without knocking.

Not understood, Moa moves along asunder,
losing the path as the daylight creeps
with shadows of departure. Distance looks Moa's way.

Now Moa's there, stoutly bringing up the rear.
Brothers, we who live in darkness, sings Harry,
let us kill Moa, push him off.

Beware the Masters of Pig Island, Moa,
and skedaddle for it from Skull Hill:
they'd make if they could a bike seat of your beak.

Upon the upland range stride easy, Moa;
surrender to the sky your squawk of anger,
and at the door of the underworld, pass in peace.

Selected Poems of Nelson Kiwi

The Bespoke Poem.

The Undesirable Poem.

The Self-Destructive Poem.

The Sabotaged Poem.

The Poem on a Suspension Bridge.

The Poem Which Passeth Understanding.

The Shipwrecked Souls Poem.

Conceptual Poem: Holding Your Breath While Humming in the Key of
    G-sharp.

Poem for the Tax Department in Lieu of Payment Poem.

The Real Estate Revolution Will Not Be Poeticised, Nor Poetry Monetised
    Poem.

The Then I Looked At It And I Was Like, Well, Actually Poem.

The Barely There, Nearly There, Only There's No There There Poem.

The Pop-Up and Quibble Poem.

The Drop Everything and Run Poem.

The Dealing with the Balcony Heckler Poem.

The Cut It Short Poem.

The Smoking Typewriter

A paper tiger burning bright,
in the typewriter of the night.
Is it a romantic or a stalker
who worships at that metal altar?

In what distant ages dead and gone
lurk those balladeers, typing on?
Crescendoes from midnight till dawn,
crisscrossed keys clacking as they yawn?

Ancient slack-jawed bards have ever,
to ting of carriage bell and whirr of lever,
tapped out peewee squibs that sputter,
and then flare out as love-lorn mutter.

With fangs of white-out and stripey smears,
as carbon copy from the roller tears:
a paper tiger burning bright,
in savage typewriter of the night.

Qwertyuiop! Qwertyuiop!

Poem for Ben Brown

Hey Ben, no matter how you jive,
you'll never get out of this poem alive.
Like Diamond Lil and D'Arcy Cresswell, Carmen Rupe,
and Uncle Scrim, and the Rawleigh's Man –
have you heard of him? –
you'll never get out of this poem alive.
You push the pedals, I'll steer, we'll both drive,
but you'll never get out of this poem alive.
Like Amy Bock's Petticoat Pioneers, Godfrey Bowen's
Click Go the Shears, Dame Ngaio Marsh's
murdering musterers;
like Canon Bob Lowe, and Tommy-boy Adderley,
Monty Holcroft, and Minnie Dean,
you'll never get out of this poem alive.
You can hula-hoop all the way to the top
of the Beehive,
but you'll never get out of this poem alive.
Like Ron Jorgensen's disappearance,
Mr Asia's debt clearance,
Phil Warren's firebombed nightclub entrance,
you'll never get out of this poem alive.
Never get out, never get out,
no matter how much you jump and shout.
Them's the breaks, them's ain't fakes,
them's knowing what it takes.
Like a roll-call of lucky beasts,
or New Zealand's surfing greats, WB Sutch,
Micky Savage, Prince Tui Teka, Lofty Blomfield,
John A Lee or JKB –
I speak on behalf of the nation,
so please refrain from expectoration –
you'll never ever get out of this poem alive.

Bruno Lawrence, Rewi Alley, Hector Bolitho,
and my Aunt Sally, Selwyn Toogood, Mack Herewini,
Possum Bourne, and Chew Chong –
they never got out of this poem alive.
Like Mother Mary Aubert, the Man Alone,
the Woman at the Store, Miss Eileen Duggan's
worsted plain, Charles Kingsford Smith's balsa
tri-plane – never get out, never get out.
Bruce Mason's fruity tones, Patricia Bartlett's groans,
Lew Pryme didn't make old bones;
the surrealistic pillow of Philip Clairmont,
the deary-me of Beatrice Tinsley,
the what's all this then of Truby King
the never mind all that of Sir Wally Nash.
Let's agree, to a degree –
you'll never get out, never get out,
never get out of this poem alive!

The Collective

a bevy of poets
a brood of poets
      a murmuration of poets
a fluther of poets
a bouquet of poets
      a lamentation of poets
a sloth of poets
a dither of poets
      an expostulation of poets
an ambush of poets
a zeal of poets
      a congregation of poets
a drift of poets
a cackle of poets
      a contention of poets
a charm of poets
a wisdom of poets
      an ostentation of poets

      – an unkindness of critics

Toss

Sir Mountford Tosswill Woollaston
painted with lightning and phlogiston.
A knight of the brush,
he parried with paint in a rush.
His clouds, heavy as wool sacks,
were formed out of clods
made in the shade,
scrubbed in the rain,
sunned in the flame,
cased in the gleam,
runnelled in the stream.
His hills were the same –
they rose from the mud,
as if flung from the hooves
of horses on courses,
or sprigs of the boots
of the mighty All Blacks.

Jamie Oliver's TV Dinner

How can I cook thee? Let me count the ways.
You've been tubbed, you've been rubbed, you've been scrubbed.
You're lovable, huggable and eatable. Get out the pots and pans.
I peels an onion; I defrosts a chook; I chops, therefore I hams.
Gather round for a TV natter. I just want to say cheese whizz.
Not Gordon Ramsay's pan-sizzled bull's pizzle,
nor Nigella Lawson's rum-soaked strawberry tart;
thumping beefcake, groaning cheesecake, reek of artichoke heart.
Lovely-jubbly, smile sugar-coated, rosy as a cherub's posterior;
bunch of carrots in one hand, bunch of rhubarb in the other.
Ritzy nosh-up with high-end bubbly, breast of roasted pigeon –
pile high the platter till the pukka tucker teeter-totters;
only remember, never eat anything bigger than your head;
never eat anything prettier than you are.
Never eat anything that just walked in and sat down in the kitchen.

Age of the Anthrocene

this is the age of the anthrocene, the anthrocene age –
an age when you want to tear the thumping
from your chest,
an age when all buses should kneel on request

this is an age of beautimus maximus bae,
an age of too long didn't read,
an age of laughed out loud till I puked,
an age of narp – not a real person,
an age of fomo, yolo, of just freakin' google it,
of good for you, and having an awky mo',
an age when all buses should kneel on request

this is an age of the training path,
the flow chart, the right road,
an age of the unsustainable doomsday factor by ten,
this is an age of planet rich, planet poor,
of planet stupid, planet more,
an age of oglebook, an age of farmageddon,
an age of lies that make baby Jesus cry,
an age of insert commercial here,
of the guilty pleasures of a Lamborghini

this is an age mocked by the trigger finger
of the hand of God,
this is an age of shanty town chic and poverty tourists,
of copper mined from Xmas tree lights,
an age of armageddonites who gather at the river
only there's no river there,
an age of child soldiers newly weaponised

this is an age to declutter and scatter ex-husbands,
an age to take a wheelie bag and a Puffa jacket
on a booze cruise,
an age of the numbing-down of airports,
an age of kleptocracy, an age of oligarchy,
an age of draining the swamp and swamping the drainage,
an age when you just cannot take
another laser beam up the jacksie

this is an age of the mischievous information cascade,
of the online disinhibition effect,
of the compulsive acronym disorder,
an age of the rumour-milled, the snapchatted,
of the emergency colours of life and death,
an age of everybody in your face,
an age of a sick, sick, sick disgrace,
of Kafka's castle, and the bull market in clover,
an age when doves are arming themselves
against the newly peaceable hawks,
an age of the metadadaist and the alarm coder,
of cybercrud and the cyber caliphate,
of cyberspies with backdoor eyes

this is an age when you need
to chow down on the feed,
an age to be offended on a daily basis,
an age of loving the long tail,
an age of elites too big to fail,
an age of psychic baggage and sinkholes,
of boneyards, scorched skin, black eclipse,
of hot tar slurry, lunar ellipse,
of rainbow spectrums and temper tantrums,
of a charter for the rights of mother Earth

this is an age of the multiplex movie End,
when lights go up and the crowd walks,
with credits music stealing through them,
making them part happy-clappy,
part-mournful, like a break-up party
where everyone has a good cry
and a final laugh,
yes, rejoice, 'cause this is the age of the anthrocene,
whether shock and awe breaking down your door,
or just the liquid mean and a twitchy dream

this is an age of bragging rights
with added acne and bad breath
of iris scanners and handprint readers,
of carbon dioxide probes and heartbeat detectors,
of just sayin' body fat is only bubble wrap,
this is an age of as you were,
      only creepier and forever,
carboniferous, saline and webcammed,
toking the smoke from burning banknotes,
an age of take it, make it, break it up again,
an age when I took the two thousand and sixteen
pieces you threw away,
and peeled off the backing night and day

this is the age of the anthrocene, the anthrocene age,
a tied-off, dried-off age,
an age when you want to tear the thumping
from your chest,
an age when all buses should kneel on request

Mission Creep

The mission creep,
the mission creep,
who can stand the mission creep,
turn creepier and creepier,
before turning completely creepy?
She creeps, he creeps, we all creep,
but especially them – they creep
me out, brother –
They are you, bro',
creepy by nature –
the missionary creep,
the bleeding edge creep,
the age creep, the rage creep,
the out of its cage creep.
The aggravations of system gamers,
bad behaviours of political party lion-tamers.
In the legislature,
who was the instigator,
the prestidigitator,
and the procurator, the promulgator,
foot flat to the accelerator?
Ask any citizen firelighter,
blurter, blogger, or tattered survivor
proud on battlements of coal-scuttle helmets.
The crude, the coarse,
and worse and worse –
you change your search terms,
but less and less emerges.
Just bitter-breathed admonitions,
and down in the trenches –
raw meat torn by bugle blasts.
Cascades of nodding poppy heads

liquefy into a river wide and red.
Automatic pilots bring the news.
Flags are placed for a bucket list
on ramparts of body parts,
with prayers over god-awfulness:
sob sister of the predator,
blood brother of the murderer.
A common deed, the bolt from the blue.
So, one more heave, weight-watcher,
because you've been randomly selected
for mission creep –
the mission creep,
the mission creep,
who can stand the mission creep?
Nah, nah, nah, nah, nah.

The Ashes Curse

I walk all over the earth.
I earth my ears to groundswell,
and hear from crusted ashes –
We will burn you and rake your ashes
into urns to shoot on firing ranges,
or in canisters be sent to outer space,
or flung to four winds, foul winds;
stench of vegetating plankton from a sea dead,
apart from plastic, jellyfish and ashes.
Never too many cadavers to bob
in life's backwash,
for no one can get away with anything –
we will remember you,
and hunt you down, or run you down,
or behead you, or revise you out of existence,
to be forever damned to oblivion,
gone to starred voids, gone to ashes.

A Rejection Ode

Obey all that oozes:
jelly ooze,
mortal ooze,
the ooze from a table of contents.
Here is the world-wide-ooze:
and he hath arisen from the ooze,
operating in a different order of reality,
a gun-crazy reality,
and the 1001 opinionated resident think-tank
pundits caught in the cross-fire,
each calling out this keyboard's for hire,
are lost in the ooze of the many –
the ectoplasm of the advert's slanguage,
the hornet of plenty's ice-cream cornet melting.
Through falling boxes of pizzas
oozes the moral panic of nations.
The ooze of oil is purified
into a monster blob of silly putty.
Flesh oozes into existence,
and all the boys and girls grieve
for the blankness of their ghost-written faces.
Here are the limited shelf-life pieces of theory,
get them while they're hot, while they ooze,
and hope they throw a long shadow.
So here we go, slipping on the barf,
on the greasy runnels of the minimum wage economy,
for which ooze –
thank the stars: thank you stars, thanks.

The People-Smuggler's Beard

There was the Brother Baxter louse-bearing beard.
Karl Stead wore a turtleneck with a beard.
How many sprouting potato-eyes to make
Sebastian Black's great beard of the 1970s?
The hog-riding biker's beard, red as summer rātā;
the rash beard; the spurious sporran;
the short beard, springy as gutta-percha.
Tartan beards of lairds; bed-cover beards;
tūī lurking in bird's-nest beards with twigs,
to chorus a bush creed for greenies.

They were the oracles of their day,
the elders who pursed their lips,
and shook their heads and faded away,
gnawing fingernails and stroking jihadist beards.
Moses, patriarch of the longhairs,
ringletted Nebuchadnezzar, Karl Marx
and his jeroboam of beard, the unshaven Shavians.
Walt Whitman's salt-and-pepper bardic chops.
Ned Kelly's stringybark face-fungus brought him down,
the false beard of Ezra Pound,
the chin fluff of incipient beardies waits to be found.
Allen Ginsberg's pubic beard in the shape of the USA,
hiding a bomb or a bicycle or a B52,
crossing the border at Mexicali;
Allen Ginsberg, alone, naked,
with knapsack, watch, camera, poem, and beard.

Plaited, pig-tailed, weedwhacking wonders;
Dundreary whiskers combed into a hairshirt.
The prickling wisp; the curly-wurly convoluted;
the spurred and booted; the deeply-rooted.

The straight Ho Chi Minh trail beard;
the Gilbert and Sullivan vaudevillian beard;
the Jerusalem syndrome redeemer's beard;
the Stockholm syndrome kidnapper's beard;
the cybercaliphate's beheaded beard.
Beards with cobwebs and rigging and cordage.
The beard in its cups, making a tingle in nostrils,
that yabba-yabba, woof-woof gurgle-beard –
because Bacchus has drowned more men than Neptune.
The desperate beard, the daily beard, the beard that disappeared.

Identity Parade

The man who fell to earth
The man who gave birth
The man who stole the sun
The amazing transparent man
The incredible shrinking man
The flying disc man from Mars
The man of a thousand faces
The man who knew too much
The man who saw tomorrow
The man who was Thursday
The man with the deadly lens
The man they couldn't hang
The most dangerous man alive
The man who died twice
The man with the oxblood leather brogues
The man who never was
The man who never returned
The man who was not alone
The man named Dave
The man in the shadows
The man who made way
The man who was in a rush
The man who mistook the moon for a candy bar –
a dream for a Cadillac,
a riverbed for a road,
a flowerbed for a home,
a treetop for a diving board,
– that man.

Scale

Jump from pram, pushchair, with excitement,
leap off springboard, vault from gymnasium,
chase along, surge away, running strong.

If you see something rising, then help it rise,
shin up the ladder, handhold and foothold,
climb through branches level after level.

Start from a standstill; be bold in movement,
a dreamer at dawn, a stepper on a treadmill,
a stair-dancer soaring on to the next floor.

Strike out for the peaks, vaulting ascender,
steady at the heels of advancing figures,
tramping before you in zigzag processional

to balconies of cloud above stepped lakes.
Go where creeks tumble, birds spiral below,
and drag of gravity rakes you earthwards.

Ascend over years, to cliff-tops and precipice,
to slips and stumbles, ever-narrowing path,
go slowly up the mountain in closing mist.

Obelisk

By the stone tower of the Anzac obelisk,
larks are ascending and walnuts descending.
Golden morning was juicy as a Packham pear,
now autumn's evening sifts its dry yellow light,
and time's gold gilt comes off in my hands.
Harping on, wasps string a lyre through gardens.
Flocks are airborne; whales spout on the horizon.
Seasons sow, ripen, harvest, and are barren.
Whiffs of river slime drift from rock snot,
and a green phosphorescent mould grows
all over my clammy, sticky fingers.
Snails' silver trails are all across leopard-print lawns.
The scratchy twigs quibble with bird song.
The hunted rook staggers from tree to tree.
Rag-winged leaves blow from stark branches.
The angry, half-inched leaf mulch
gets up and totters away, buzzing.
A mountain's cracked cauldron steams.
Somewhere north, a chuckling creek
drowns the rain-gauge
and fleeces float to the waiting sea.

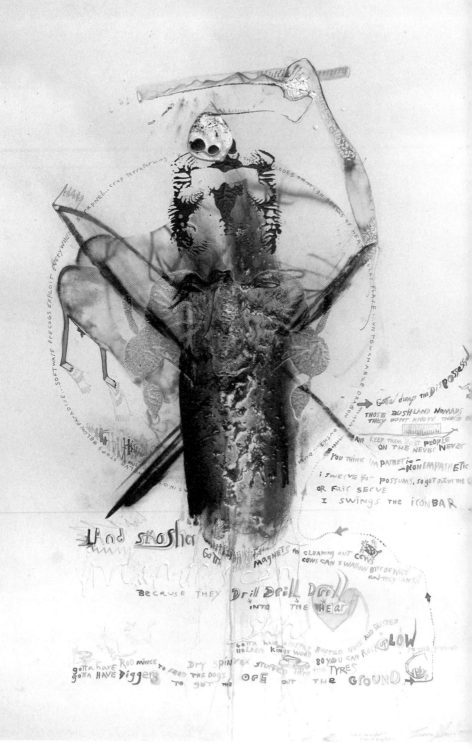

PART FIVE: LEGEND

With Woven Mats

With woven mats
my muse's bedroom
is an albatross nest,
where she contemplates
the moons of her nails.

Love Bite

She fills his heaven,
rocks his world,
oils his wheels –
then shoves him under …

Men's Group

He's a marooned kingpin
inside a circle of empty chairs,
ripping away the silver lining.

He has risen shriven
from his wicked sins,
a freedom camper unbound.

He has a watching crowd of disbelievers.
He hiccups his way
through a recital of misfortune.

He has the unction of an undertaker.
He takes the measure of warmth
to be found in a shot glass.

He wears a number of competing deodorants,
his head has the glossy sheen
of a recently polished doorknob.

He's the mute witness.
He's been consuming up large since forever.
He grubs the same ground over.

His language is lickerish, bootylicious.
He raises a cloud of insects,
and is admired by a tūī, a tomtit and a rifleman.

He fudges whether he has ever served in the SAS.
He is absolutely sweet and choice,
and off to bro' repairs.

My Inner Aotearoa

My inner Aotearoa is smoky blue gums
in a corner of the khaki paddock,
a crunching noise underfoot from withered grasses,
        the tarred road bleeding in the sun,
        creek beds shoaling as a dusty river,
        bush decked with trails of clematis flowers.
When I only had gorse in my pockets,
I went in fear of the spiralling arms
of Crab Nebula, somewhere overhead.
Now I escape to stamp the black bubbles
of hot bitumen as if treading grapes,
and run headlong up Breakneck Road.

My inner Aotearoa is a need to brake
to descend the incline,
and I want it steep, steeper, steepest.
        A riddled leaf smites my wet cheek,
        a hailstorm of lies
        is illuminated in a lightning flash.
A glacier shrinks to the size of an ice-cube,
to be crunched, steadily.
But dig deep, deeper, deepest,
throw up topsoil till it rains potatoes.
The magnitude of the extra grunt
resounds, as one more raindrop falls.

My inner Aotearoa is a lake's rise
and fall, a heartbeat.
The transcendental meaning of flesh
is raised on a bier,
        on a balsawood cross,
        on a barbecue grill,
        on a hospital bed.

Light thickens and sours in the milk bottle,
glugs heavily in the sinkhole,
leading to the place where all sinkholes empty.
So just hold your nose and jump,
into eternal darkness made visible.

Thirty Days of Night

Night, as the last amber drains from heaven.
Night, as I dip my quill into a dark pool and begin.
Night, as an earthquake trembles a chandelier.
Night's coal hulks rotting at anchor.
Night's coal heaver,
glow-wormy, tattooed with blue light.
Night's Bible, leather-black
and gold-tooled, on the table.
Night, little worms of flame
shooting through blackening pages.
Night beyond the black sump,
the wallow, all the yackety-yak.
Night's trouble of fools,
watching while the colour of night rages.
Some new-fangled thing or other,
made of fire and night.

Night over crosses in cemeteries,
over glimmers of hospitals, auto-wreckers' yards.
Night's fingers that tap the steering wheel.
Night's zoo beasts that nag neighbourhoods.
Night's siren, as if a rabid banshee
has gone off-slope to echolocate down a canyon.
Night hiding the secrets of the chic
in their thready suits.
Night, removing sock-shod feet
from yawning shoes.
Night, and those awful black briefs.
Night, alive and tarry, and entering on tippy-toes.
Night knows what it wants,
it wants nocturnes fried in grease.
Night that grabs you by the lapels
at the edge of the abyss.

Night's chiaroscuro crumbled to charcoal.
Night, and the black gorge flash-floods,
to sluice across tapu ground.
Night, where the express doesn't stop.
Night, a stab in the dark,
under the Dog Star.
Night, a lonely shout into the thunder.
Night that archives itself in stealth
inside the history of shadows.
Night that weighs its grams, grain by grain,
out in a golden balance.
Night, as if a nameless rogue, a fugue,
as if no, nil, nix, not, never.
Night bells for the dying and the risen again.
As mica glitters in schist, so hoar frost night.

The Great Wave

There is no god but God, go mongooses in the monsoon.
The rains thrum on empty biscuit tin drums
to rattle Suva market and flick your face.
The jail's walls are ivory; a rainbow crooks an elbow.
The old shoeshine boy begs for money
for a cup of tea and two pieces of bread.
Everybody wears jogging shoes and sneakers,
the jingle-jangle of the bangle-seller is drowned
by a radio that could walk five hundred miles,
and then go walking on the moon to a bass line by Sting.
A crimson hibiscus lei drapes the punchbowl
at the bar, where I renovate my inner temple
and wait for the night to extend my winning streak,
as hotel staff slice tops off fresh pineapples
to reach garlanded pinnacles of mirrors.
A hinge bends to lift a drift log from the surf.
Thus spake Zarathustra to the fa`afafine:
bruise me with purple shadows of evening fallen
over searched caves of eyes that lids close on.
I listen to the ocean chant words from Rotuma.
The *Mariposa* is a butterfly between islands.
A heatwave, fathoms green, whose light spreads
its coconut oil or ghee or thick candlenut soot,
twinkles like fireflies over plantation gloom,
and heart's surge is the world's deep breath.
I learn to love every move the great wave makes;
it coils you into each silken twist of foam,
blown far, all the way to salt-touched Tonga
with mango pits, wooden baler, shells awash.
My uncle, swimming from New Zealand, wades
out of the sea and wades onshore at Levuka,
where my grandmother is staring out
from her hillside grove of trees waiting for him.

Orbit of the Corpse Flower

'That corpse you planted last year in your garden,
Has it begun to sprout? Will it bloom this year?'

(T.S. Eliot: *The Waste Land*)

Botanical voluptuary, the corpse flower rises
like an idol, like Houdini in a green shroud,
from its flower altar, pungent as a body farm
for rookie detectives, bringing all the flies
in Christendom, though they can't get in;
it unfurls its frilly reproductive parasol
behind glass in Dunedin's hothouse jungle,
while our creeping queue curls out the doors,
and each of us stares, massed like forest
come to Dunsinane, at the force whose fuse
both blooms and withers in a moment, a day;
each sniffing carefully to classify the stink
from the catalogue that makes olfactory memory,
orange fish swimming below in their pool;
enclosure within enclosure, closet within closet,
and within the smallest closet this cuckoo-clock.

Above sea-fog, holding cruise ships off-shore,
the sun's a furnace stoke-hold elevated,
the expanse unfurling its risen temperature,
while algal blooms thickly on all the phosphates,
the wind carrying remembrance of things dust,
Radiance of the Sea's horns serenade the harbour,
and on a dry night what sounds like rain
is an ovation from Forsyth Barr stadium
as 'Dark Side of the Moon' by Roger Waters ends,
so we reach for the supermoon to touch only clouds
on tip-toe, not the low-hung rim with fingertips,

weightless, bodiless, boneless as moon shadow,
for the bounce of that sailing basketball is
slam-dunked elsewhere by other star-gazers,
before the next colossal *Princess of the Sea* arrives
and a brawl of waves at St Clair spills on-shore.

Bagpipe chanters, ding-dong clappers, egg-beater's
overhead clatter down to land on hospital helipad,
bellbirds unfurling at dawn with tintinnabulation,
monotonous palavers heard round the Octagon,
amid spires, turrets, stacked stone of kirks,
cast-iron's fence-top dirks, summer clearances;
all warming to rattle of hail on slate, frozen music,
smell of burnt coffee and buttery cheese rolls;
then the sea blows its salt into our nostrils,
scent of fresh sawdust, turpentine, blackberry jam,
milk on the turn, burnt rice, smoke of joss sticks,
old wet macs drying as if decomposing,
grim contents of a long-disconnected fridge,
noses twitching at crotch and armpit musk,
Saint Valentine found suffocated by rose petals,
corpse flower in swoon at its own aromatic cosmos.

Escapologist

They locked him in a prison van.
They kettled him in a milk can.
They entombed him in a block of ice.
They shackled him to a truck chassis twice.
They bound him to a windmill vane.
They dropped him down a cannon with a crane.
They padlocked him inside a mailbag.
They sewed him tight to the American flag.
They roped him high on a skyscraper girder.
They lowered him in a box in New York Harbour.
He escaped them all, the Great Houdini.
He took on fake psychics; he challenged spirit mediums.
He fought hypnotic swindlers and their bogus accomplices.
He exposed them all, the Great Houdini.

She was trained in the art of séances.
She regurgitated ectoplasm and went into trances.
She rapped with spirits by cracking her toe joints.
She made ghost noises and threw male voices.
She tapped, and a table tilted, a chair fell over.
She shook, and a shellac record slowed on a Victrola.
She used her elbows, and moved things with her knees.
She hung in the darkness from a trapeze.
She was the mind-reader, Mina Stinson Crandon.
She declared her psychic powers were outstanding.
She believed she was a match for Harry Houdini.
But her apple sauce and her way with the cha-cha
did not impress the Great Houdini.
She levitated on wires, she swayed around.
He always kept both feet on the ground.
How the crowd roared and cheered for the Great Houdini.

Legend

When the word was god,
each god-bothered poet knelt
within a nexus of traumas –
for flesh began to write on clay,
producing a coinage of psychodramas
to blotch tanned, toughened animal hide,
as the butterfingered held their tongues
and preachers prayed into cupped hands.

When the word was god –
Aleph, Eleah, Ilos, Dios, A`a –
praise song erupted, sacred drums talked,
and sunbursts sought explicators.
The starry abracadabra of alphabets,
carved out of ancient groans and grunts,
found fountains of ink to guide blood feuds
onto parchment with flying feathers.

When the word was god,
palimpsests sprang up under erasers.
Melismas gathered and sang to lutes.
Out of cradles half-strangled boasts
offered primal and talismanic syllables;
then uttered arpeggios began to peal,
chiming, effortless; then impromptu oaths
rang out in rugged strophes and staves.

When the word was god,
the muse was a statuesque reader,
who read by light of her own pale brow,
as poets painted each toenail,
her poetic foot in battered sandal.

They conjured her as an odalisque,
and with traceries they pressed lips
to cavernous ears to whisper hopes and fears.

When the word was god,
the first maker of the first ode
arose anonymous, another god,
epic enabler of voices of the outlawed,
of the sly bawdries of the banished skald,
of the divine chants of the vagabond scribe,
of the saturnine namesakes of nemesis,
of the unsayable being said over and over.

NOTES

Some of these poems have been previously published, or have appeared elsewhere, and acknowledgements are accordingly made to the following: *Broadsheet*, Dunedin Public Libraries, *The Café Reader, Cordite, Flash Frontier, Ika, New Zealand Books/Pukapuka Aotearoa*, nzepc, *Otago Daily Times*, Otakou Press, Phantom Billstickers, *The Press, Poetry New Zealand, Percutio, Takahe*, the Spinoff.

I wish to thank the University of Otago and the Wallace Arts Trust for the James Wallace Residency at the Pah Homestead in Auckland in late 2013, when early drafts of some of these poems were produced. The poem 'Phantasmagoria from Mount Victoria/Takuranga, Devonport' was begun while I held a short-term residency at the Michael King Writer's Centre in Devonport in April 2009, and completed in April 2016. The financial assistance of a Creative New Zealand Toi Aotearoa Quick Response Grant in late 2015 was instrumental in the draft preparation of this manuscript.

A number of poems were first trialled in draft form at poetry readings, and acknowledgements are due to the Octagon Collective and the Dog with Two Tails Café, Dunedin, and Poetry Live at the Thirsty Dog Tavern, Auckland.

The poem 'Moa in the Mātukituki Valley: A Cento' incorporates lines and phrases from poems by the following poets: James K. Baxter, Thomas Bracken, Charles Brasch, Ursula Bethell, Alistair Te Ariki Campbell, Allen Curnow, Eileen Duggan, Denis Glover, A.R.D. Fairburn, Cilla McQueen, Bill Manhire, Owen Marshall and Hone Tuwhare.

In this book I have elected to use the term 'anthrocene' as more mellifluous and less tortuous in preference to the more commonly used 'anthropocene'. In 1992 the science writer Andrew Revkin, in his book *Global Warming: Understanding the forecast*, speculated about what earth scientists might name the post-Holocene age: 'We are entering an age that might someday be referred to as, say, the Anthrocene. After all, it is a geological age of our own making.'

The poems 'Panel Beater', 'This Gubberment, Bro, This Gubberment', 'Penny Serenade', 'Planet Blast', 'Land Smasher' and 'In Crematoria' were written as a

Six Sonnet sequence in 2015 in response to seeing artworks by James Robinson, which he produced on a 2014 Dunmoochin Foundation artist residency near Melbourne in Victoria, Australia. The Six Sonnet sequence was exhibited as a set of drawings by the artist at PG gallery 192 in Christchurch in August 2015.

The cover image is the artwork assemblage 'Utopia's Mines' (2014), produced by James Robinson when he held the Dunmoochin Foundation residency. I am grateful to Marian Maguire and PG gallery 192, Christchurch, for providing the image. All the drawings are by James Robinson, courtesy of PG gallery 192.

Special thanks to Ben Brown for his off-the-cuff 'write five poems in five days' poetry challenge, which led to 'Poem for Ben Brown'.

I would also like to thank the following for inspiration, support and help in putting this collection together: Fieke Neuman, Glen Eggleton and Terence Rissetto.

I am grateful for the perspicacious questions, the attention to detail and the care shown by this book's editor, Emma Neale, and all subsequent confusions are to be laid at my own door. Thanks, too, to my publisher at Otago University Press, Rachel Scott, for ongoing support.

Edgeland desire lines, grasshopper sususrrus, clatter of trains, chatter of magpies, now.
– Robert Macfarlane

Leave the door open for the unknown, the door into the dark.
– Rebecca Solnit